TIGRESS *at* FULL MOON

Obiwu

AFRICAN HERITAGE PRESS
New York • Lagos • London
2012

AFRICAN HERITAGE PRESS

NEW YORK
PO BOX 1433
NEW ROCHELLE, NY 10802
USA

LAGOS
PO BOX 14452
IKEJA, LAGOS
NIGERIA

TEL: (Toll Free) 855-247-7737; 914-481-8488
FAX: 914-481-8489
Email: afroheritage9760@aol.com
www.africanheritagepress.com

First Edition, African Heritage Press, 2012

Library of Congress catalog number: 2009931551

Obiwu

Cover Design: Dapo Ojoade

Distributors: African Books Collective, www.africanbookscollective.com

ISBN: 978-0-9790858-4-0
ISBN: 0-9790858-4-5

Dedication

For Adaobi, Akuobi,
and their mother, Ifeyinwa

Contents

Preface vii

Path One: Intimations

Tigress at Full Moon. 3
Her Eyes Were Watching God 4
Bloodline. 5
Between the Stop Sign & the Bullet 6
Secret Soldiers 8
A Man of Good Taste 9
The Deadline. 10
O-b-a-m-a! 11

Path Two: Laughters in Thunder

Bone Depot 15
Her Flesh is Wild 16
Dangerous Ground. 17
Babambe 18
Old Niger Runs Through It 19
The Undertaker's Smile 20
Bless the Child. 21
Beauty 23

Path Three: Epigramatics

Syracuse 27
Snowhill 28
Slow Fire. 28
Sullen Snake 28
Head Over Heels in Louisiana. 29
Bono's Brain 30
Museveni Monologue 31
American Democracy 32

Path Four: Babel

Ukwu Bü Otu 35
E Pluribus Unum 36

Nnukwu Öha 37
The Big Crew 38
Ala Na-Ama Jigiji 39
Ground Dey Shake 40
Amüma Mmiri 41
Water Maid. 42
Ïgba Afa Eze Dibia. 43
The Chief Priest's Invocation 44
Uge. 45
Libation 46

Appendix: Select Critical Reception on *Rituals of the Sun* (Poems, 1992)

Obiwu's Agwu and Other Gods of Poetry 49
By Ben Obumselu, D.Phil. (Oxon), Professor Emeritus

The Agwu Trinity in Obiwu's *Rituals of the Sun* 51
By Afam Ebeogu, Ph.D. (Ibadan), Professor and Dean,
Abia State University, Uturu, Nigeria

Glossary of Igbo/Nigerian Names and Terms 57
Acknowledgments 63
A Note on the Author 67
Comments on the Poems of *Tigress at Full Moon* 69

Preface

Across centuries and vast geographic regions the Nazarite warrior, Samson and the British solitaire, William Blake variously confront the terrifying beauty of the tiger. In culture, politics, and mythology the tiger remains the mega-fauna of greatness and power. In triumph or loss, the tiger always defines itself. Its generic representation as *Panthera tigris*—"all" + "beast"—depicts the tiger as the omnipresent master of the animal space. The same dialectical genome signifies the feminine species as tigress. What is beyond the supreme matriarch of the jungle in fending for its cub or fending off the anamorphic gaze of the evil eye? In comic pseudo-culture, Tigress is an alpha huntress who is both sinned and sinning, heroine and hounder perennially preoccupied with the vagaries of justice and balance of power. Tigress manifests the multi-variant incarnations of the Igbo Pantheon of gods, spirits, gnomes, myths, nymphs, and legends—like *Agwü*, *Ögbanje*, *Kamalü*, *Ekwensu*, *Ikenga*, *Ökpösï*, and *Mammywöta*—as shown in the undulating phases of *Tigress at Full Moon*.

In the continuing tumult of hope and change in a globalized world, *Tigress at Full Moon* is conceived as affirmative responses to primal and primary desire. The volume responds to elegiac interventions in contemporary human, economic, and global warming upheavals like genocide, war, terrorism, hurricane, earthquake, desertification, hunger, disease, and migration. It responds to private and communal carnivals as much as to mundane and cosmic catastrophes. Barack Obama's quip to his chief strategist David Axelrod after his loss of the New Hampshire presidential primaries, "I think we were flying too close to the sun, like Icarus," overdetermines the Achebean schema on the cosmic complications of excess.

When a son sues in open court against the sacrilegious overreach of his own father who ravishes his wife with presidential gratification or when a daughter bewails her psychosocial diminution by her own father's incestuous rape in pre-puberty, it revivifies the archetypal "father of the horde" as the persistence of an insidious death-wish in *pari passu* with the Sophoclean and Freudian-Lacanian imaginary. Plato's *Euthyphyro* (in which Euthyphyro sues his father for impiety) and

Christopher Okigbo's "Elegy of the Wind" are backdrops to the scandals of "Bloodline," "A Man of Good Taste," and "Her Flesh is Wild."

Tigress at Full Moon is a totemic offering to the failure of *jouissance* and to the swing-state moods and tempests of the citizens, the nations, and their seasons.

Obiwu
Wilberforce/Xenia, Ohio

PATH ONE

Intimations

A nation and a woman are not forgiven the unguarded hour in which the first adventurer that came along could violate them.

—KARL MARX

Tigress at Full Moon

Response to Chimamanda Ngozi Adichie's Half of a Yellow Sun

Like red wine in a full glass
Everything is visible to the eyes
We behold the object of adoration
Like an enchanted archipelago

The moon at night is sedate
We feed our hearts in her strawberry bowl
The tang sweetness is the blessing of roses
Prickly and soft as petals and thorns

Starry eyes are mediated columns
Milky Way of polyvalent monocles
Thunderous rage, lightning rumbles
Cowry shells in plaintive chants

Here is a regal tigress at full moon
Here is a rampaging *Agwu* that plows her chambers

Her Eyes Were Watching God

For Katrina & Tsunami, Response to Zora Neale Hurston's Their Eyes Were Watching God

Taut, the molten stirred
She saw the force
The power of God
In her eyes
The tumult of His strength
A quivering arrow
His thrust was potent
Her eyes were watching God
Her blood roused
Like melting flesh
She felt the storm
Exploding hurricane
And foam-white surges
Oh, God!

Bloodline

Response to Edwidge Danticat's The Farming of Bones

> *All great, world-historical facts and personages occur, as it were, twice: the first time as tragedy, the second as farce.*
> —Karl Marx

Introit:
There is a farming of bones
Where Ogun is feasting at dusk

He hanged his father
He strangled his mother
He stood on their graves
And smiled at his work—

I am Olumo

I am my father's
My father is mine . . .

He yelped at the moon
And pranced on the rock

His victims assail his dreams
His dreams impair his sleep
He stabbed his wife
Then he banished his son—

I am Aso

I am my son's
My son is mine . . .

Between the Stop Sign & the Bullet

Response to Bianca McGuire's "Little Hope"

She stood at the podium, and
Her voice rose in song, of
The one who was caught
(Without drums or cymbals)
Between the stop sign & the bullet

She counted a grocery list of
Cars, clothes, drugs, guns, jewelry, money, pussy
And whatever counted in the
Bling and smoke of the
Street where she grew

He was one of the many she
Had loved, who slipped through
Her life like the million wayward sands
That ran through her fingers
At the neighborhood playground

She stood, medium height
Mahogany hue, gold-brown hair
Dancing fingers that played an
Imaginary piano; neither her
Smiling eyes nor the gentle
Gaiety of her slight frame could
Betray the pain that
Seared her youthful flesh
Her woman's body which
Bore the burden of blighted males

Her fingers played on invisible keys
Her entrapped audience swooned in
Chorus of the one who was known as
Brother, cousin, father, uncle, husband, lover, son
All boys buried before they became men

She stood firm at the podium
Her defiant voice rose in praise of
The men of her youth, playground mates
Weightless males who were caught
Between the stop sign & the bullet

Secret Soldiers

Response to Achebe's Things Fall Apart

If I hold her foot
She says, 'Don't touch!'

Spritely heels, mists of
Secret soldiers
And incandescent butterflies

Wraps are for rifling, son
Oats thrive
In the Sahel, not in Sahara

Hunger, like a bull or ram
Rushes headlong
Faster than her victim

Passion pines, reason runs
Chambermaid of
Half-light dreams, lo!

When I hold her waist-beads
She pretends not to know

A Man of Good Taste

Response to Christopher Okigbo's "Fragments Out of the Deluge"

> *"The oral poet," she said to him teasingly. "Show me what an oral poet can do." And he laid her out, lay upon her, put his lips to her ears, opened them . . . showed her."*
>
> —J. M. Coetzee

He put his mouth where his money
Was, and he grew a swollen snout
Slurred speech, woodpecker syndrome
He-goat who ate the yam in his care
His mouth was evidence he was led
By his nose, as the flies flew, he went
Saw, ate. He drenched his loins, licked
His snout, thrust his skynose face for
All to see, that he was a man of his
Word, a man of good smell and taste
Oral-driven, who went, saw, ate
And grew a swollen snout

The world was witness to his bravery
His good taste, his orality

The Deadline

Response to Tupac's "That's Just the Way It Is"

Between you and me we draw a line
Sheep and cattle do not mix—
We draw a line between north and south
We draw a line between man and woman
Black and white are colors of death

My brother draws a line on our land
This line is a fence, he says—
Across distances of rage and fear
Thrusting fingers flare like fires
We curse and yell at high-rise walls

The mosque is a line before the church
Cross and crescent do not mix—
Dagger is a mark; bullet is a point
Blood is water; men are sands
We raise arms; we shun words

Pundits draw a line between two worlds
Light and dark; good and evil—
We spy each another through looking glasses
We stretch arms across open spaces
The leg that crosses the deadline dies

O-b-a-m-a!

Where he treads, there is halo
With each step, the ground shakes

Winds wave
Crowds rise
Hands clap
Calls hail:

O-b-a-m-a!
O-b-a-m-a!

Tides rise and grow
Reeds pave his path
Lights usher him
Sounds echo him:

O-b-a-m-a!
O-b-a-m-a!

Prince of radiant sun and shrine
Bulls throng behind him

PATH TWO

Laughters in Thunder

The bleeding phallus
Dripping fresh from the carnage cries out for
the medicinal leaf . . .

—CHRISTOPHER OKIGBO, "ELEGY OF THE WIND"

Bone Depot

Underneath the breadfruit tree
Between the pear and the papaya
Tens of old and scattered mounds
Low round heaps of bushy earth
Space unmarked by stone or stick
Biafra's babies starved and strafed
Buried bodies bound and bombed

Fathers and heroes and tribal lords
Promise keepers and scorpion chiefs
Their dreams were deadlier than daggers
Their eyes were fiercer than ferrets
Their words poured like poisoned rain
Between the yard and the grave
Between the homestead and the wasteland

Her Flesh is Wild

"Your flesh is wild," he said
He looked into her eyes
He saw her gaze in his eyes
He drew her down upon the grass
Above them droned the din of turbulent clouds

She crooned of men and miseries
Of disasters under the matrimonial sheet
An incestuous dad and a faithless spouse:
"Like the dust of history, Lord
Let this cup pass over me
Let me know the beauty of your face
Variegated rose and sunflower"

She looked into his eyes
He could feel the pulsation of her blood
Her heart beat riotously like war drums
"Before the sun should set," she yearned
"Let my blood draw every breath of this land
Let me die in the heat of your flesh"

Images skeined the presences of his past
A life he had known, a world behind him
Inch by inch, ashes of broken angels
Yard by yard, wrecks of maniacal leopards
Between the swamp and the desert
And a mother's ghost crying for help

"The flesh is willing and the will is firm," he wailed
"Let me drink of the berries of the wild
Let my blood run wild in your veins
To this land I belong, to this land I return
I bring the sceptral powers of my race"

She cuddled him with a victory smile

Dangerous Ground

For Hembadoon

A private path
Is a public track
When the market is full
Of parts and parcels

We haggle
You and me
Across open wares
On public display

We rise to dins
And swells of the market
And lock arms as strangers
Caught in rabid passions

When is a part not a path?
When is a trace not a track?

Babambe

It was an alluring fruit from which I could not draw my eyes. I went for it, but my hopeful hands beheld a sponged emptiness. I tore into the marshy mess with the savagery of my clawed fingers. My teeth bit into my excited tongue. I felt what the Christ must have felt on that day of killing-hunger, when he lashed the mocking-fig on the road to Salem. "Every tree that bears no fruit shall. . . ." How could it be, I wondered, that in a desert of barren dust the only thing that looked alive was not really different from everything else? "Welcome to the desert of the real," cried Zizek, who must have seen what I saw. That wild fruit was *babambe*, an empty fruit. It grew among the Margi of Madagali below *Tudun Mandara*. That was before Google and Yahoo!, uncouth weirdo of Adamawa! Yet, like the echoing angst of Euclid's stone, I could not help but feel it again—the bewitched tenderness, the excruciating and ocular deception of my once lovely *babambe*.

Old Niger Runs Through It

He could have loved the moon
But distances assail him
Like ripened nuts between scraggy thorns

She could have loved the sun
But distances assail her
Like thirsty tongues between skynose hills

Great Wall is long
Eiffel Tower is high
Grand Canyon is deep

Ochanja heat grows and spreads
Old Niger runs through it

The Undertaker's Smile

For Ezenwa-Ohaeto, Michael Mbabuike, and Don Ohadike

> *'Stetson!*
> *'You who were with me in the ships at Mylae!*
> *'That corpse you planted last year in your garden,*
> *'Has it begun to sprout? Will it bloom this year?*
> *'Or has the sudden frost disturbed its bed? . . . '*
> —T. S. Eliot

At the Speedway door
Comes the undertaker
Charmer at a gas station
"Hello" was his smiling eyes
He must have known me
Or had seen me before
A familiar face, another body
At a funeral table
Shaved, washed, and
Dressed for the solemn throng

I knew him too
We knew each another
Body and undertaker
Subject and predicate
We meet as he leaves the Speedway store
His funeral home a breath away
He clasps his cappuccino cup
And says "Hello" with a widening grin
I say "Hello" with a sporting smile
And go for my cappuccino cup

We met once
Now we meet
Before the supperless dinner
At a funeral table

Bless the Child

For Adaobi, January 13, 2005

Bless the child

Visitor at dawn
Father, mother
Path to the spring
Or to wood gathering
Froth of palm wine
Flowering oil bean
Sensations that simmer
And jolts of blood that linger

Bless her who comes
In the name of the father
And the mother's tears
That speak her father's name
In a land unloved
Birds unbeaked
Songs unsung

Unbidden guest
Unhosted traveler
Sojourner and wanderer
Intertwined cones
Of violent love
And tender hate

Bless the child, land
The Mobius Serpent
That coils on itself
Tail in its mouth
And tongue untied
Like a poisoned arrow
Drawn to snap
And feed on its own womb

Bless the air, sea, plants
Beasts, dead, living
And bless the infant traveler
And the land that lies in ruins
Like a patient glory
At the gates of iron history

Beauty

I
Beauty is the air I feel
In the velvet swoosh of your voice
That lingers in my ear through the
Placid lullaby of the telephone when I'm
Wrapped in the warm caress of
Your nectar—the oil bean flower plucked
On the narrow path of *Opara* spring

II
Love is your gaze
That drives flaming embers
In perfect oblivion of cold nights
When I swim in the sheets of your
Embrace, your thighs that sing and
Hands that pull strings over threnody—
Pipe dreams blossom in tangible forms

III
Your kiss calms as autumnal air
Your laughter pushes back the night
Your feet glide as fish in tide
Your eyes are windows to my heart
Your hair, hips, lips, and breasts
You are a collage of dreams—
In light or dark you will be loved

PATH THREE

Epigramatics

Stretch, stretch, O antennae,
to clutch at this hour,
fulfilling each moment in a
broken monody.

—CHRISTOPHER OKIGBO, "WATERMAID"

Syracuse

Broad arch
Salt Mountain
Where you spread
I place
Intertextual
Word on warm ice

I bow and tremble

Snowhill

The snow of Syracuse does not dance
To the drums of the weatherman

Slow Fire

Slow fire of smoldering desert;
Scattered bones of yesterday's romp

Sullen Snake

Sullen snake that swallows his kind;
Shallow earth that beckons to them

Head Over Heels in Louisiana

Hey, I can see land!

Screams the president on Air Force One
His sweaty palms cusp breast-curtains:

This Katrina is not deep;
Let's go back to Washington.

Bono's Brain

The dark face of the sun
Is a place of savagery—
People live there
People are dying . . .

She responds, pen on inkpad:
We're in a place of lack
Of deprivation, of absence
This is the dead land

Museveni Monologue

In Biafra
Five of ten children died of kwashiorkor
In Ruhiira
Four of ten are chronic and dying . . .

He responds, stirring his tea:
Burnt grass
That's what ruhiira means
That's what ruhiira means

American Democracy

> *I never had no interest in [presidential elections] because my vote don't matter anyway . . . knew white people had the right of way here . . . gonna get me a ticket [for Inauguration Day]? . . . I'm ready.*
>
> —97-year-old Mother Brew of Washington, DC

Minority will have its say
Majority will have its way
Alterity will have its day

PATH FOUR

Babel

We have a language which is so efficient in its structure
that some say it was first spoken in Eden.

—MICHAEL J. C. ECHERUO

Ukwu Bü Otu

Maka nwa öhïa, ngözï, June 7, 2007

Anyanwü k' ïbü
Önwa k'ïbü

Ï bü nnukwu üha
Nö na Önü Agwü
Anyï eweta ihe ïchu aja gbara ibe
Ökükö öcha, ebule oji

Kpakpando k' ïbü
Si na-ala
Si na mmiri
Si na ikuku n'ökü
Igwe mbara bu nku abadaba
Anya ele mie
Ntï agbatïa
Enyunyo asaa ka osimiri

Ï bü onye Amerïka
Onye oji, onye öcha
Onye Biafra, onye Jew
Ukwu bü otu

Nrö k' ïbü
Üwa k' ïbü

E Pluribus Unum

For the exile, a baptism, June 7, 2007

Sun you are
Moon you are

You are giant *üha*
At Önü Agwü shrine
We bring twin totems
White chick, black ram

A star you are
From the earth
From the stream
From wind and fire

Wide skies bear broad wings
Eyes strain far
Ears grow long
Sea-wide stretch of shadows

You are American
Black, white
Biafran, Jew
E Pluribus Unum

Dream you are
World you are

Nnukwu Öha

Ebe özörö ükwü, ebube adï
Ükwü özöla, ala amaa jigiji

Öha ebilie
Aka na-akü
Oku na-akpö:
Nnukwu Öha!

Ikuku mmiri too ya ebuo
Achara atüö üzö osi aga
Ihe akpöbata ya
Üda akpökuo ya:

Oke Öjï
Igu Ehime
Ichie
Nna

Ökpara anyanwü ihe na ülö aja
Enyi kwü ya na-azü

The Big Crew

Where he treads, there is halo
With each step, the ground shakes

Crowds rise
Hands clap
Calls hail:
The Big Crew!

Tides rise and grow
Reeds pave his path
Lights usher him
Sounds echo him:

Big Iroko
Ehime Stone
Ancestor
Father

Prince of radiant sun and shrine
Bulls throng behind him

Ala Na-Ama Jigiji

Otua ka ozi si abïa
Ala na-ama jigiji
Ihe n'eme na California
N'eme zi na Illinois

Enyi m bi na Chicago
Ya na ndï be ya
Ozi na-abïa
Onye öbüla n'ekwu
Ndï mmadü na-atü egwu
Ükwü n'eji

Anya nö m n'onyoonyoo mgbasa ozi
Ntï m n'ege ntï
M'abïa n'eche
Gïnï n'eme na Chicago?
Mmadü önwürü? Ülö ödara? Ügböala ökürü?
Achörö m ïkpö enyi m

Aka m ji igwe ozi
M'ana ele onyoonyoo mgbasa ozi
Onyoonyoo mgbasa ozi n'ele m
Ntï m nö ebe dum
Igwe ozi önwüöla ebe ahü?
Ka m buru-üzö detuo ihe a

Ihe n'eme na California
N'eme zi na Illinois
Ahü m na-ama jigiji
Ala na-ama jigiji

Ground Dey Shake

Na so news dey come
Ground dey shake
Di tin wey dey hapin for California
Don dey hapin for Illinois

My friend dey live for Chicago
Him and him family
News dey come
Evribodi dey talk
People dey fear
Leg dey crip

My eye dey tv
My ear dey lisin
I come dey tink
Wetin dey hapin for Chicago?
Person die, house fall, moto crash?
I wan call my friend

My hand hol telefon
I dey look tv
Tv dey look me
My ear dey evriwere
Telefon don die for yonda?
Make I fes write dis tin down

Di tin wey dey hapin for California
Don dey hapin for Illinois
Bodi dey shake
Ground dey shake

Amüma Mmiri

Ezigbo m
Echiche gï n'echu m üra

Olu mgbaba-azü gï
Ükwü ï zörö n'ala
Ibe ji önwa dï gï n'obi
Bü ihe-eji arö nrö

M'ödïghï ihe özö i mere taa
Amüma mmiri m
Biko, sutu enyunyo m önü

Water Maid

My beloved
I long for you

Your sonorous voice
Your feet on the ground
The twin moons on your chest
Are the stuff of dreams

If you did nothing else today
My flashlight beauty
Please, give my portrait a kiss

Ïgba Afa Eze Dibia

Ahaziri ya n'olu egwu nke African American "Hoochie Coochie Blues"

> *Eze dibia ülö aja agbööla üja*
> *n'okwu ebube*
> —Christopher Okigbo, "Elegy of the Wind"

> *Onye gburu dibia na-agwörö ya ögwü, ndï na-agwörö ya nshi agwü chaa la ha?*
> —Igbo proverb

E ji m öfö
E ji m ogu
Ükwü üsü anya pïara
Eze abü n'eji oji
E ji m obi ödüm n'abüba ugo
Anya nkïta n'ele enwe
A ga m emegï-ihe

The Chief Priest's Invocation

Set to the cue of the African American "Hoochie Coochie Blues"

The chief priest of the sanctuary has uttered
the enchanted words
—Christopher Okigbo, "Elegy of the Wind"

He who kills his medicineman, are all his poisoners dead?
—Igbo proverb

I got a ritual staff
I got a piercing spike
Blind-bat foot
Black-cat tooth
I got lion's heart and eagle's feather
Dog's eyes watch the devious monkey
I'm gonna mess with you

Uge

Obi udo nd'ije duwe gï

Obi udo ilö üwa duwe gï

Obi udo akö n'uche duwe gï

Obi udo ihe n'itiri duwe gï

Obi udo öfö n'ogu duwe gï

Obi udo ökü na mmiri duwe gï

Obi udo elu na-ala duwe gï

Ïga-aga m'öbü ïlö alö
Anyanwü-Okike, önwa, na kpakpando
Üzö nkü n'üzö iyi
Üzö ömümü n'üzö mmüta
Üzö mmüö n'üzö mmadü

Obi udo ndï ichie duwe gï

Libation

Spirit of peace of travelers guide you

Spirit of peace of reincarnation guide you

Spirit of peace of wisdom and thought guide you

Spirit of peace of light and dark guide you

Spirit of peace of staff and spike guide you

Spirit of peace of fire and water guide you

Spirit of peace of heaven and earth guide you

Going or coming
Creator-Sun, moon, and stars
Path to wood and path to spring
Path to birth and path to knowledge
Path of spirit and path of human

Spirit of peace of ancestors guide you

APPENDIX

Select Critical Reception on *Rituals of the Sun* (Poems, 1992)

Obiwu's Agwu and Other Gods of Poetry

By Ben Obumselu

Reading a new poet is like travel in a strange country. The roads are unfamiliar; the neighborhoods are unknown. Occasionally we may hear the note of joy or exasperation in the cadences of our guide, but we are not to grasp his meaning. The large building whose red roofs and curtained windows rise besides the streets, are they palaces, warehouses, or prisons?

But not knowing where we are is the exhilarating experience for which we come. We are tourists because we are connoisseurs of the unfamiliar, going out to meet whatever is counter, original, spare, or strange not just to question it but also to question the familiar contours of our own lives.

At the centre of Wole Soyinka's poetry there is the strange god Ogun, creator and destroyer of life. In his rocky shrine virgin blood has to be poured out, a deity not unlike the Greek Dionysus whose Euripidean legend Soyinka adapted. But we do not know this Ogun, and our curiosity about him takes us through the deeply foliaged woods of Soyinka's poetry.

Christopher Okigbo too takes us into a strange country where the river goddess Idoto, a number of Christian divinities, and the mad man Jadum preside. In the introduction to *Labyrinths* Okigbo further tells us that all his work describes the ordeals of a religious initiation which is partly a call to the poetic vocation and partly the discovery of a new life.

Obiwu's *Rituals of the Sun* will remind the reader naturally of Soyinka and Okigbo. The sun in Obiwu's title is the god Apollo in his most ancient guise as an American Indian or an Egyptian god, the source of all life and energy whose ritual is sometimes a holy sacrament on the bestial floor. Like Soyinka and Okigbo, Obiwu assimilates this god to a Nigerian counterpart, Agwu, whose three-fold revelations inspire the citizen, the madman, and the sage.

But poetry does not produce these strange gods merely to mystify us. Every archetypal wonder is evoked in order to re-kindle our living relationship with familiar things. Dionysus, the sun god Ra, Ogun, and Agwu are extrapolations from common experience. Insofar as they are symbols, we might wonder who they are and what they mean. But the experience does not lie in the symbol; the symbol lies in the experience. In Obiwu's work, as in Soyinka and Okigbo's, poetry exercises two of its oldest powers. It awakes the imagination by creating a mythical world in which the figures of romantic legend live their enchanted lives. At the same time it reclaims and vivifies the world of daily routine by renewing our grasp of its underlying meanings.

There is however a due to be paid. Each reader must read the poetry patiently, going through each poem several times and returning later to confirm his impressions. It is like getting to know the topography, the manners, and the language of a strange country. And every tourist has to do that for himself.

The Agwu Trinity in Obiwu's *Rituals of the Sun*

By Afam Ebeogu

Rituals of the Sun (1992) is assembled in three sub-divisions by the author: Part One subtitled "Agwu of the Pathways," Part Two subtitled "The White Sun," and Part Three subtitled "The Rising Sun." Crusading through the parts is a poet-persona who metamorphoses from a mere Agwu protégé to an Agwu essence itself. Agwu of course is the Igbo dualistic deity attributed both with eccentricity, at times bordering on pure madness and clarity of vision that could be quite reconstructive. In Igbo metaphysics, there are three types of Agwu which can result in diverse behavioral manifestations whose nomenclature reflect their Agwu connection. These three main cosmogonic types are the Agwu Nsi which is the patron deity of the malignant *Dibia*, often referred to as "medicineman," whose ritualistic competence includes the ability to prepare some talisman (*ogwu* or *nsi*) which could maim, cause insanity, or even kill. There is also the Agwu Afa, patron to all the *Dibia* who are essentially diviners. To them the culture assigns the divination responsibility that not only takes them into the recesses of the past for communion with the ancestors in order to dig out what has occasioned some dislocations of the present, but could also propel them into the future in a quest for assurances and cautions which the present again needs for purposive existence. Lastly, there is the Agwu Mkpologwu, mkpologwu ("roots") being a synecdoche for all herbs which Dibia Ogwu, often called "Native Doctor," uses for preparing his medicine for all types of diseases.

Now, any protégé of Agwu is said to be "possessed" by the deity, and at the initial manifestation of the possession the victim usually begins to behave abnormally. Once proved by divination as chosen by Agwu he or she must undergo some rituals of spiritual transition, before a state of near normality could be restored. Thereafter the person is initiated into the right category of Agwu discipleship to which he or she belongs. For the rest of the person's life, he or she is a protégé of Agwu and the kind and quality of service which the person renders to the society, that is, whether malignant or benevolent, would depend on the nature of the person's Agwu. Agwu is thus dualistic in manifestation not only as a culture-type in general but also in the individual. Like Ogun of the Yoruba, it is as destructive a deity as it is creative: its eccentricity ranges from ordinary mischievous pranks to outright malevolence or sublime benevolence.

It is this Agwu spirit that is at the centre of Obiwu's *Rituals of the Sun*. The poet bestows it with an epic stature, and its journey from "Agwu of the Pathways," to "The Rising-Sun" is symbolic of and parallel to the poet's development from a state of dim awareness and taciturn invocation to that of explosive vision and consequent unapologetic ventriloquism. The indebtedness of this poetic scheme to the structure of Christopher Okigbo's *Labyrinths* is all too apparent. But Obiwu's structural vision cannot be described as imitative, for the association of the growth of an artist from tentative, cautious steps to confident weighty threads with mythical heroic voyage has remained a recurring phenomenon in the history of aesthetics. What has happened is that it has been the lot of the individual artist to dig out from the aesthetic universe of his culture the suitable heroic and symbolic equivalents in this mythic schema. In Part One of *Rituals of the Sun*, the mythic figure is an Agwu protégé who, in "Exordium," drinks the pristine ritual waters of the Heavens with the following invocation:

Oparaeligwe
Soothe my thirst
Cleanse my smears
Purify my mind
And make me ready
For rituals of the Sun.

Thus, spiritually and artistically cleansed, the poet-persona now steps foot on the path of creative adventure, which is also a path of the truth that the ancients "had trod before," and which the moderns of the present and future will continue to pass, as the next poem, "Okike," affirms:

The Word on marble of creation
The beginning, the present, the future
Mundus ad infinitum.

"Agwu of the Pathways" features twenty-two poems all of which in one way or the other reinforce the theme of getting into a state of preparedness for the "good poetry" so lyrically articulated thus in "Nature Music":

> Good songs are cut on slabs of time
> Every stroke clear as spring water,
> Every word precise as an archer's arrow
> Dancing in the eyes of the sun.

That, i.e. "good songs," is the poet-persona's aspiration which he is as yet to achieve. For the moment, he is only sensitive to an overflow of impressions—"crouching tatters of discordant strains"—which "suffers inhibitions/ And bears quantums/ Of discordant tones" ("Labyrinths" 12). He needs proper guidance in this task of poetic evolution, and one is not surprised that the various mentors that urge him include a mythical old man's voice "deep from the dim" ("A Voice in the Night" 13), and a timeless vision of fair lady ("Fair Lady" 16) who, in "Counterpoint" (18-20), a poem of impressive metrical experimentation in which a narrative contour is structured into a rhythmic interchange between the protagonist (labeled Man), his inner voice (labeled Mind), mother of the lady in quest (labeled Face) and of course the poet-persona who narrates the incidence, becomes the persona's lover. It is the same "fair lady" and lover who metamorphoses into a proper name—Vivian—in "Sunflower" (23), a poem in which the woman's wavy and flowing hair assumes the mythic spread of the sunflower, metaphor for beauty, light, and love

Indeed, the metaphor of light, often represented by the image of the sun, is very strong in Obiwu's poetic sequence. It symbolizes immortality often evoked in many of the poems, as in "Namuluna" (24) where Onyaagu reminds us of the "watery presence" of Okigbo's Idoto. Not even the momentary interpolation of such poems as "Broken Monody I" and "Broken Monody II" (26-27) which portray a sense of catastrophe, of unrelieved pain, is able to destroy this image, and it is significant that, in "Broken Monody II," "our famished laughters/break in sunlight" (27). And this is because the poet-persona is an Agwu protégé, and Agwu is still in control. Though a "messenger of Wrath" and "bleeding sword of warriors," he is also a "harvester of fruits of seasons," "sower of seeds of farmlands," "ripper of buds of springtime," and "strong arm of farmers" ("Agwu" 30). Here, the link with Ogun in Soyinka's famous "Idanre" is extremely suggestive not only of the archetypal stature of Agwu but also of young Obiwu's indebtedness to the elder poet.

As we move into the ten poems of Part Two, subtitled "The White Sun," it becomes clear that the poet-persona's state of spiritual and creative apprenticeship has gone beyond the early neophyte stage. These are poems which, though they still feature the uncertainties and hesitancies of the earlier protagonist, strongly anticipate redemptive possibilities. The first poem in this section, confidently titled "Voice of Thunder" (35), is subtitled "For the Untitled." Obviously, the Agwu protégé is becoming "half-Agwu" and feeling himself almost like a fulfilled initiate. The fact that the poet-persona's voice is stronger in this section is reflected in the strong presence of a social consciousness in the poems. For example, the poem "Scrambling Affair" (36-37) is a strong portrayal of the deceit and profligacy characteristic of Nigeria's political elite. The voices in the poem are "scrambling" voices, adequately captured in a "scrambling rhythm" in which the political instability and malpractices of the nation are quite effectively presented in a metrical graphetics. And the protagonist is sure that vengeance, coming like "flying arrows," will be visited on these mismanagers of leadership ("What the Oldman Said" 38). The poet-persona is not afraid to affirm his role as a supersensitive artist who must talk even when others keep silent, and, in "Invocation" (41), he ritually takes an Ogun-like oath in the fashion of a warrior set for battle. In "The Dance" (48), this Agwu-suffused protagonist makes it obvious that fear is not to be associated with him: come peace come violence, he is all for action!

The third part of the volume, "The Rising Sun," containing seven poems, features not just an Agwu protégé, but a protégé now metamorphosed into the Agwu deity himself. Not surprisingly, the persona is now full of strength and wisdom, and this is reflected in his recourse to proverbial expressions much of the time. Understandably, therefore, the poems are not just talking about mundane action and destruction, but of the infinite beauty and eternal repose which is the future. This is a triumph of poetic wish fulfillment which is the stuff of which the mythic imagination is made. In "The Brand" (56), a ritualistic poem promising us Love and Life in capital letters, the

Agwu essence begins to merge into one with the personality of the poet; hence the ritualistic branding in the piece is administered to the poet by his grandfather, who was "an ancient medicineman and an Ogbanje" (56). In "Dedication" (59), the protagonist affirms that he is "sacred and profound," and proceeds to identify himself with diverse facts of the deities and philosophers of the past, represented by Njoku on the one hand and Sartre and Nietzsche on the other. "Song of a Village Minstrel" (60-61) presents him as a full initiate; the Agwu himself! According to him:

> I have danced
> In the world of spirits
> My friend,
> I have danced
> In the world of men,
> And can tell
> Why a millipede
> Cannot dance,
> Though it has a thousand feet (60-61)

Not surprisingly, that last but one poem of the collection, "Song of the Time" (62-67), finally hammers down the identity of the persona as that of the poet: the persona is identified as Obiwu, the poet, and he salutes his audience in a typically panegyric format characteristic of African self-praise poetry. The piece is full of historicity and social vision, and the poet identifies his ancestral source and the various parts of Nigeria which have informed his experiences. Ultimately, he affirms himself as a kind of mythical savior in these lines:

> I, Obiwu
> I am the prophet of life and the future
> Ours is a past of dead Sun
> Ours is a present of dying Sun
> Our future's sun shall be immense and sublime (66)

The sun image, promising eternal sublimity, which runs through the whole poems of the volume, perseveres to the end. *Rituals of the Sun* is scintillating to read; it is impressive in conception and style.

Through the use of private and archetypal images personal experience is made to assume mythic dimensions. Some of the poems, like "A Grief Ago" (42-46) and "Counterpoint" (18-20), are quite metrically experimental and effective.

One of the major problems facing any poet-beginner, especially if he is using free verse, is that of determining the pause boundaries of each line. Obiwu tackles the problem by preferring to stick much of the time to natural syntactic units determining his lines, without sacrificing the essential presence of poetic rhythm. His images are fresh and striking, though the extremely secretive nature of some of them can distract in the process of interpretation. It could be argued that the echoes of some of his influences, like Okigbo and Soyinka, are at times too obvious for comfort, and this is an area which the poet has to pay greater attention to in the future. It is, however, clear that there is a discernible personal voice in this collection, and *Rituals of the Sun* can be considered a successful volume, especially as a first outing.

Glossary of Igbo/Nigerian Names and Terms

Abü
Bush cat; cat. Variations: bush cat—abü; cat—nwa aküko, nwa aköm, nwa mba; See bush baby—nwa anwashï.

Agwü
Igbo god of madness and creativity; god of poetry, music, and oracles; god of artists, diviners, and warriors. A distant relation of the Greek god Apollo. Three authorities emphasize the god's threefold personalities and manifestations: patron deity of evil "medicinemen," diviners, and native doctors (Ebeogu); primary deity of the medicine man, fortune tellers, and often misidentified with the god of evil—poison (Echeruo); inspirer of the citizen, the madman, and the sage (Obumselu). See extended clarification in Obumselu's "Obiwu's Agwu and Other Gods of Poetry" and Ebeogu's "The Agwu Trinity in Obiwu's *Rituals of the Sun*," both included in this volume. See Michael J. C. Echeruo's *Igbo-English Dictionary* (1998), Obiwu's *Rituals of the Sun* (1992), and Chinua Achebe's *Anthills of the Savanna* (1987).

Amüma Mmiri
Lightning; flashlight. Metonym of breathtaking beauty. See Mammywöta, mermaid, and "water maid" below.

Anyanwü-Okike
Creator-Sun; Creative Force; God's eye. Variant: *Iwu Anyanwu.* A distant associate of the ancient Egyptian Sun-god Ra and the Greco-Roman Apollo.

Aso
Monolithic historical landmark in Suleja/Abuja (AKA "Zuma Rock"), which also marks the official residence of the Nigerian presidency.

Babambe
Margi/Hausa word for "empty fruit."

Ekwensu
Igbo god of mischief and confusion. Trickster spirit. It is a distant kinsman of the European Mephistopheles in Christopher Marlow's *Doctor Faustus* (c. 1589, 1593) and Goethe's *Faust* (1808). Unlike the Christian fallen angel, Ekwensu is the ever present companion and Achilles's Heel of success and confidence in Igbo cosmology.

Enwe
Monkey

Eze Dibia
Chief priest; lead medicine man

Ichie
Ancestor; also term of endearment for an elder who is by his or her advanced age always already a link, conduit, intercessor, or intermediary between the worlds of the living and the undead, the earthly and the ether, the mortal and the immortal. See *nna* below and the *egwugwu* scene in Achebe's *Things Fall Apart* (1958).

Igu Ehime
Ehime stone or rock; site of the originary, evolutionary myth of Ehime's founding father and mother

Ikenga
Igbo gnome, emblem, or symbol of the right arm/hand, strength, and abundant harvest. See Achebe's *Arrow of God* (1964).

Ïgba Afa
Divination; consulting the oracle; invocation

Ilö Üwa
Reincarnation

Kamalü
Igbo god of thunder and lightning; god of fire

Mammywöta
Mermaid; "Water Maid"; water woman; spirit of the sea. Its religious followership across Igbo land is known as Owu. Its biannual ritual festival is celebrated in the town of Umueze II (Umuezeowere), Ehime Mbano, by the *Owu* Masks, and in Umuahia (Ndume) by the *Daa Mgborie* Masks. See *amüma mmïrï* above.

Margi
Language and people along the foot of the Mandara Hills between the Northeastern Nigeria and the Cameroons.

Ndï ichie
Elders; ancestors

Niger
Iconic River Niger and historical landmark of the fabled city of Onitsha in Southeastern Nigeria. Both city and river are twin totems, patron-saint, and muse of Nigeria's first president Nnamdi Azikiwe (Zik) and his poetry.

Nkïta
Dog

Nna
Father; ancestor. See also *ichie* above and the *egwugwu* scene in Achebe's *Things Fall Apart.*

Nnukwu
Big; huge; gigantic; large; many; very significant; a very important person; one man squad; E.g. Igbo: *Otu onye anasï "unu abiala"* ("One person to whom is said 'Have you all come?'"); US: "An Army of One."

Nshi
Poison; charm, magic, and evil divination. Dialectal variant: *nsi*. See also *anwa nsi*—magic, necromancy.

Ogu
Ritual spike, wand, emblem, verge, rod, symbol of innocence and guiltlessness.

Ogun
Yoruba god of creativity and destructivity. See Agwu above.

Oke Öjï
Big or gigantic iroko tree; ageless iroko tree. Suggests both the tree and its metonym as praise name.

Olumo
Mythopoeic Olumo Rock and historical landmark in Abeokuta, Southwestern Nigeria.

Öchanja
Fabled Onitsha market, one of the busiest and biggest in Nigeria, on the eastern flank of the mythopeic River Niger.

Ödüm
Lion

Öfö
Ritual staff; individual and communal idol, wand, emblem, verge, rod, symbol for the pursuit of truth; authority and power through truth.

Öfö n'ogu
Ritua staff and ritual spike; wand of innocence and truthfulness as metonyms of authority and power. As idiomatic collocation the two go hand-in-hand, one with and to the other rather than side by side.

Ögbanje
Spirit-child; one bestriding the earthly and ancestral domains, the living and the undead worlds. See also Achebe's *Things Fall Apart*.

Ögwü
Curative medicine; divination

Öha
Kinsfolk; community; extended family; public; crowd; gathering. See Hawaii *ohana*.

Ökpösï
Carved ancestral gnome, verge, or wand; ancestral emblem or symbol of self and communal protection.

Ökpara
First son; prince. Dialectal variant of *öpara* below.

Önü Agwü
Agwu shrine of Ezeowere (AKA Umuezeowere or Umueze II) town of Ehime Mbano, site of the biannual Owu Mermaid Festival. Its totems are the *üha* tree, chick, and ram.

Önwa
Moon; feminized metonym of woman's breasts or "twin moons"—*ibe ji*

Öpara
Short for *Öparaeligwe*; twin spring waters and their Sky-Prince god, marked by monolithic rocks and potassium, and foliaged cove of ancient trees, lying between the three communities of Ezeowere, Eleke (AKA Umueleke), and Ezeama (AKA Umuezeama or Umueze I). Dialectal variant of *ökpara* above.

Tudun Mandara
Mandara Hill/Mountain on the border of Northeastern Nigeria and the Cameroons

Ugo
Eagle

Üsü
Bat

Acknowledgments

The critical reference to Plato's *Euthyphyro* in the Foreword is owed to the editorial disquisitions of Professor Lee Ingham of Central State University, Wilberforce, Ohio.

Epigraphs to Path One and "Bloodline" are from Karl Marx's "The Eighteenth Brumaire of Louis Bonaparte," *The Marx-Engels Reader*. Ed. Robert C. Tucker. New York: W. W. Norton, 1978.

The line and poem title, "Between the Stop Sign & the Bullet," is from Bianca McGuire's unpublished performance poem, "Little Hope."

Italicized lines in "Secret Soldiers" are from Chinua Achebe's *Things Fall Apart*. New York: Anchor Books, 1994.

Epigraph to "A Man of Good Taste" is from J. M. Coetzee's chapter on "The Novel in Africa," in his novel *Elizabeth Costello*. New York: Viking, 2003.

"O-b-a-m-a!," "American Democracy," "The Deadline," "Head Over Heels in Louisiana," and "E Pluribus Unum" were published in *Fieralingue*, Nov 22, 2008, as part of "While the He/Art Pants: Poetic Responses to the 2008 American Elections," at: http://www.fieralingue.it/corner.php?pa=printpage&pid=2709 (accessed 22 Nov 2008)

The epigraphs in Path Two and "Ïgba Afa Eze Dibia"/ "The Chief Priest's Invocation" are from Christopher Okigbo's "Elegy of the Wind" in *Labyrinths: Poems*. London: Heinemann, 1971. Path Three epigraph is from Okigbo's "Watermaid" in the same anthology.

The line, "Welcome to the desert of the real," in "Babambe," is from Slavoj Žižek's *Welcome to the Desert of the Real!: Five Essays on September 11 and Related Dates*. London: Verso, 2002.

"The Undertaker's Smile" was originally published on *Kwenu.com*, January 31, 2007; and in *Dialectical Anthropology*, 31.1-3 (2007):

331. Epigraph to "The Undertaker's Smile" is from T. S. Eliot's "The Burial of the Dead" sequence of *The Waste Land*. Ed. Valerie Eliot. New York: A Harvest Special—Harcourt Brace Jovanovich, 1974.

"Beauty" was originally composed as a Wordsworthian "visionary gleam" of the tigress at full moon whose sophomoric promise was foreshadowed in Okigbo's "Love Apart": "two pines/That bow to each other . . . /But kiss the air only."

Italicized lines in "Bono's Brain" and "Museveni Monologue" are from Nina Munk's article, "Jeffrey Sachs's $200 Billion Dream," in *Vanity Fair* (July 2007).

Epigraph to "American Democracy" is from the elderly African American Patti Brew, whose vote for Senator Obama on November 4, 2008, was her very first in a presidential election in nearly a century. See Gillian Gaynair and Brett Zongker. "Americans Rush Plans for Obama Inauguration." *Yahoo! News-AP* (Nov 24, 2008). http://news.yahoo.com/s/ap/20081124/ap_on_go_pr_wh/inauguration_american_stories;_ylt=AvWQkXYpu9Q3aHdexCIqylKyFz4D (accessed 24 Nov 2008)

Path Four epigraph is from Michael J. C. Echeruo, *A Matter of Identity—Aham Efule: Ahiajoku Lecture*. Owerri, Nigeria: Ministry of Information, 1979. Poems and translations in Igbo have further assistance from "The New Standard Orthography" in Echeruo, *Igbo-English Dictionary: A Comprehensive Dictionary of the Igbo Language with an English-Igbo Index*. New Haven, CT: Yale UP, 1998. Okigbo's "Love Apart" is cited from Echeruo. *A Concordance to the Poems of Christopher Okigbo (With the Complete Texts of the Poems, 1957–1967)*. Foreword. Isidore Okpewho. Lewiston, NY: The Edwin Mellen P, 2008.

"Ground Dey Shake," pidgin version of "Ala Na-Ama Jigiji," was originally webshopped on the three premier global listservs of Nigerian writers (*Krazitivity*, *Josana,* and *Ederi)* as a ricochet on the momentous hazard of a rare 450 mile radius 5.2 magnitude earthquake (April 18, 2008) to which residents of Illinois and environs were exposed, with the gaze on the family of a friend Okwudili Okeke.

"The Big Crew" and "Libation," English versions of "Nnukwu Öha" and "Uge," were conceived as dialectal oral performance pieces—in call-and-response format—for the enhancement of folk traditions in the African Diaspora, though they can easily work well in other non-African settings. The words, names, and images—as is usual with the oral performance genre—are metonymic and therefore transferable and substitutive according to gender and situational needs. They were first presented in a wake observance for an Igbo elder Odogwu Öranaekwulu Ösakwe (*Nkwü Amawbïa*), on Saturday, April 26, 2008, at the St Georges Episcopal Church in Centerville, Ohio. I could never have suspected the conflicted response of the audience to my introduction of our (Ahmed Kadiri for the English, I for the Igbo) recital as an *Ama-ala* traditional rite of passage. A terrible choice of words under the circumstance! Some Igbo-Christian audience members seemed affronted as forced-witnesses to "a heathenist ritual" which they had presumably escaped as American sojourners and exiles. It was a bizarre irony that both versions of "The Big Crew" met with greater success as part of the July 5, 2008, tribute to the 25th priesthood anniversary of the Reverend Father Emeka Linus Iwuanyanwu at the Holy Rosary Roman Catholic Church in the Bronx. (Obiwu. "The Names of the Father." In Emeka Iwuanyanwu. *Silver Jubilee Celebration*. Bronx, NY: Kola Print, 2008. 10-14) The New York acclaim affirms the validity of both poems as panegyrics, elegies, or dirges at celebrations, milestones, and rites of passage, including wedding, baby shower, christening, birthday, graduation, housewarming, dedication, thanksgiving, eulogy, and transition ceremonies. This explains the substitutive experimentation of "O-b-a-m-a!"

Ben Obumselu's "Obiwu's Agwu and Other Gods of Poetry," which is published in full here for the first time, is the original introduction to *Rituals of the Sun* (1992).

Afam Ebeogu's "The Agwu Trinity in Obiwu's *Rituals of the Sun*" is the first official review of *Rituals of the Sun: Poems*. Kaduna, Nigeria: Klamidas, 1992.

Ahmed Maiwada's blurb citation on "The Undertaker's Smile" is from Henry Akubuiro, "Judges Who Gave Sefi Attah Soyinka Prize Are Mediocrities (sic)." *Daily Sun*. March 25, 2007. http://odili.net/news/source/2007/mar/25/802.html (accessed 25 March 2007)

A Note on the Author

Obiwu received his Ph.D. (with distinction) in English with emphasis on Critical Theory from Syracuse University, Syracuse, New York, and wrote his dissertation on *In the Name of the Father: Lacanian Reading of Four White South African Writers. Tigress at Full Moon* is his second volume of poetry since *Rituals of the Sun* (1992). Obiwu's other publications have been widely acclaimed. He won the Donatus Nwoga Prize for Literary Criticism in Poetry (2009) with his essay on "The Ecopoetics of Christopher Okigbo and Ezra Pound." He was a fellow of the Presidential Leadership Institute, Central State University, Wilberforce, Ohio (2011) and a fellow of the International School of Theory in the Humanities (1998). His other awards include the Charanjit Rangi Leadership Award for Faculty Professional Excellence from Central State University (2008) and the Resolution Recognition (No. 07-4-12-31) from the Greene County Board of Commissioners of Ohio (2007). Obiwu teaches English in the Department of Humanities, Central State University in Wilberforce, Ohio.

Comments on the Poems of *Tigress at Full Moon*

Agbaza! Obiwu's "Ground Dey Shake" is what we called poetry before the *oyinbo* man came and called us backward illiterates!
—**Ikhide R. Ikheloa**, Essayist and Bureaucrat

I marveled at the composition of Obiwu's "The Undertaker's Smile." If I am to pick the five all-time best poems in Nigeria, I will include that poem alongside those of Soyinka and Okara.
—**Ahmed Maiwada**, *Daily Sun*

I am scared of encountering a tigress at full moon. I am thrilled by Obiwu's metaphor.
—**Amanze Akpuda**, Editor of *Reconstructing the Canon*

I enjoyed the subtly cutting irony and witticism of Obiwu's "A Man of Good Taste." Brilliant!
—**Uche Umezurike**, Author of *Dark through the Delta*

Obiwu's "Between the Stop Sign & the Bullet" is an absolutely wonderful piece."
—**Olu Oguibe**, Author of *The Culture Game*

In a word, Obiwu's "Her Flesh is Wild" is brilliant. Somewhat redolent of "Sunflower" (in *Rituals of the Sun*) but more extended, and definitely light years away in maturity. More please.
—**Helon Habila**, Author of *Waiting for an Angel*

"Bless the Child" is a beautiful poem that recalls the golden opportunity I had in encountering the best published poet of the University of Jos (Nigeria), my favorite poet Obiwu! His *Rituals of the Sun* is so evocative that one feels like one is reading Christopher Okigbo. I found in him the difference between a born poet and a charlatan! Obiwu's poetry is the secret discovery I made during one of my usual visits to the Arts Section of the Unijos Library years ago!
—**Isaac Attah Ogezi**, Author of *The Misfits*